Effectuationism Philosophy-Physics (E P-P) (Oct 2020)

Grand Cohering Theories

By
Peter Kinane

Copyright © Oct. 2020

By O'Bhríd Press, c/o Peter Kinane

All rights reserved. Without limiting the rights under copyright reserved, no part of this publication may be reproduced or transmitted, in any form, or by any means, electronic, mechanical, photocopying, recording or otherwise without the publisher's prior consent in writing.

Series ...

Revised Edition: ISBN: 978-0-9954548-8-0

O'Bhríd Press, c/o Peter Kinane

Rep. of Ireland

Chat via: philosophy peter kinane e p-p blog.

CONTENTS

1. Preface
2. Introduction
3. Philosophy Overview
4. Effectuationism Philosophy System (E-PS)
5. Effectuationism Grid System (EGS)
6. 29.May.1919 Sun Eclipse and Hyades ...
7. **Emergence- -Electro-magnetism- -Gravity**
8. Mathematics
9. ECCE
10. Grand Cohering Theories
11. Monetary and Trade Theory
12. Scans

Cue: Most people require trendy cues for higher intellect to exert.

Preface

As a teenager in 1970, Classical Philosophy, expressing in my culture, did not make good sense to me. I perceived a logic-leap. I felt there was a reason for everything; that value- -decision emerged through tension of indefinite- -dynamic factors- -'forces', multifaceted.
Value: indefinite- -dynamic and multifaceted.

But my culture featured Plato's "One" - Father Supernatural - emanating static, ideal value and about which all people identified with each other- universal identification.

Its interaction with indefinite- -dynamic Mother Nature-value was incoherently defined, generating the mind-body problem for 2,400 years - one amongst many of Classical Philosophy - and pretty much conceded by Plato (428-7 – 348-7 BC) writing the Phaedo, speaking through his character Socrates: "Rather than try to give all sorts of reasons for **different phenomena**, Socrates suggests that **in the poverty of our ignorance**, we should just cling to the hypothesis we have, **the theory of Forms**, and rely on that for **our explanations**".

I baulked- -paused at this non-true-to-life and incoherent logic-leap in the formulation of the nature of things.

After twenty five years of thinking for myself, noting data of interest to my project, Effectuationism (E-PS) emerged.

I first published it in Jan. 1996 and made it available that Jan. to an international conference. Many slightly revised, more polished versions followed since and recent ones included other subjects such as Physics. (See: Index).

Specialists in philosophy immediately felt the light; felt a giant leap for Philosophy (Scan 2) but also that it was rudimentary, was formulated by someone outside of their Platonic Cave and implication that their profession had for 2,400 yrs., now embarrassingly, endorsed and promoted Bronze Age primal senses--intellect-informed (non)sense.

It quickly became trendy to rudely discuss it, **subject unstated**, in my presence, effectively precluding me from right of reply, e.g. to point out that they were (moronically) hybridizing it with their primal intellect baggage.

These Scholars of Ethics apparently lacked the spine, grace, integrity to their profession and love of wisdom to openly comment on it. Perhaps concern for their love of power and prestige took priority over good of the world.

I suspect some tried to have it, uncredited, inform, **e.g.**, the political world: In the 1990s it might have been a factor to confidence that democracy could immediately feature in non-democratic countries, even ones with conspicuous factions, categoricalist and unaware of E-PS.

If so, they could not even do that competently.

I began to bring E-PS to bear on other sciences.

As the Index indicates, it informed an alternative grid system to Einstein's Theory of Special Relativity.

It also informed an alternative to his General Relativity, which latter is a major problem for coherence of Physics.

It also addresses Emergence and the nature of Gravity.

It coheres with Quantum Dynamics and **should inform a modelling.** This is apparent in its First Principles:
Second Principle: "Effect, through, and indeed as, tension of relationship of 'forces', indefinite- -dynamic and inferentially multifaceted". (Effect: verb, non-referring).

I developed free of decades of memory cramming and of the tyranny of orthodoxy. This facilitated freedom to consider the connotations of orthodox data- -concepts rather than prioritising their memorisation and recall.

This book is the evidence!

Socrates, long before being sentenced to death by hemlock poisoning, in 399 BC when things were not going well for Athens, for both corrupting the minds of the youth of Athens and for impiety:
"The unexamined life is not worth living" and
"I know nothing [categorically]".
Unfortunately he was not advanced enough to know he was baulking at Categoricalism, without having conceived it as a system nor even conceived: System.

Introduction

This book ranges across two thousand four hundred years.

Where one starts is where one finishes; what goes in is what comes out.

So it is important to check back a long way on premises if one is interested in the rigour of one's premises, concepts, and the system they comprise and open to a profound reset.

Along the two thousand four hundred year way,
each scenario; each set of tensions of 'forces',
how they resolved,
became a factor in (mis)determination of the next 'forces'.

'Forces' in tension resolve, remaining indefinite- -dynamic.

Nature features a reform character, or reset potential; boom and bust nature; trial and error nature; indefinite- -dynamic, multi-faceted Nature.

Potentially you will undergo a profound reform as you read.

Effectuationism (E-PS) exclusively expresses Mother Nature - one exclusively am expression of Mother Nature.
Father Supernatural does not feature.
So, classical incoherent dualism does not feature.
E-PS is democracy, diversity and nature friendly.
There is potential for harmony in the soul and in the world.

Through becoming high-inferential, one becomes a more high-inferential factor to determination of evolving Mother Nature, making Mother Nature more high inferential henceforth.

Philosophy Overview

People continued to write on Philosophy-Physics for 2,400 years, because they were not happy with the sense emerging.

Concepts did not fit together as coherent and true-to-life.

Why did (academic) philosophers fail for 2,400 years?

Their **premises** were informed by intellect of the primal senses – sight, sound, touch, taste and smell - through which **concepts** express as of independent phenomena, of definite boundaries and unchanging essence – in effect, as categorical; absolute; without qualification.

They still ring a bell with people's primal intellect.

Under pressure to be fluent in orthodoxy, writers became programmed with categoricalism and focused on tweaking it, in accomplished style. They lacked the high inference development and time opportunity to consider connotations of its concepts and to check back a long way on its premises, to see the, to use Plato's words, "poverty of [] ignorance" premises.

Primal Premises Brain endured, utterly blissfully ignorant!

So it is important to check back a long way on premises if one is interested in the rigour of one's premises, concepts, and system – the software between one's ears - and open to a **profound** reset - as distinct from an MPhil or PhD.

Each scenario; each set of tensions of 'forces', how they resolve, become a (mis)determinant in the next set.

Tweaking concepts may make them more coherent and inter-flattering but **does not effect – cause to emerge - that they comprise a system and does not generate new premises, which then inform new concepts and new system.**

Academic philosophers remained trapped in a conceptual framework- -system featuring the concepts Truth, Knowledge, Fact, Reality, etc., never even becoming aware they were so trapped nor of the concept "System" nor of systems in tension testing rigour of premises, concepts, systems and resolving. Their premises and concepts would **not** feature in a new system.

What is a "System"?

Flat Earth Cosmology was a system.

A new system emerged - the Helio-centric Cosmology – and, through the two in tension, the former became apparent as a system.

Then, in tension with each other, the tension resolved - one thrived and the other declined.

There was no cross-over of concepts between them – no elephants holding up the world and causing earthquakes when they became restless, no sun-boat bringing back the Sun at night to the place from whence it riseth or new Sun being born each day and no walking over the edge of the world in the new system. **Instead, momentum and undefined gravity featured.**

In tension with each other, one thrived, the other declined.

So, **Effect- -rigour of value, through tension of 'forces'; not through inter-flattery of concepts nor through theory 'and' observation, which tends to be circular- -inter-flattering.**

Plato produced a philosophy system, premising matter as composites of 'the four elements' and without soul or intellect – without life or consciousness.

Today the notion of matter as "the four elements" and as inanimate and unconscious would be controversial, if not ridiculous.

He went outside of Mother Nature and theorised Father Supernatural through 'which' he had "soul" and "intellect" emanate ... out of (the) One, and, with increasing degree of removal, express less of the (light of) One – are less beautiful.

E-PS features life and consciousness inherent in Mother Nature.

There is no cross-over of concepts between E-PS and Categoricalism- -Classical- -Conventional Philosophy.

Let's be very careful not to hybridize E-PS, so that in tension with Categoricalism it can have a fair chance of thriving.

So, summarizing:
Concepts are system particular!
They do not translate or transfer across systems!
A system of concepts becomes apparent as such when a new one emerges; becomes apparent in tension with another.
Rigor of a system emerges through how it fares in tension - inter-relationship with any other system.
One thrives, the other declines.

A system may emerge through high intellect exertion.

C.A Qadir cites *The Madhyamika School of Sunyavada*:
"the knower, the known, and knowledge are interdependent".

The Carvaka: "The soul is but the body characterized by the attributes signified in the expressions, I am stout, I am youthful, I am grown up, I am old, etc. It is not something other than that body".

Plato (428-7 – 348-7 BC), writing the Phaedo, **talking through his character Socrates**, speaks to the effect: "Rather than try to give all sorts of reasons for **different phenomena**, Socrates suggests that **in the poverty of our ignorance**, we should just cling to the hypothesis we have, **the theory of Forms**, and rely on that for **our explanations**".

Note: **"the theory of Forms", a "hypothesis", "cling to", "in the poverty of our ignorance"**!

Credit to Plato for openness about his premises and to Socrates for his love of wisdom - he choose death over renouncing his opinions, such as: "I know nothing [categorically]".

However, it appears, such qualities were lost along the way.

Plotinus, perhaps relying on the oral medium for his information, tells us in "On Intellect, Ideas and [Real] Being": Plato regarded matter as lifeless and unconscious - without soul and intellect and that:
"Perhaps, therefore, it is ridiculous to investigate whether intellect ranks in the order of beings; ..." -
if soul and intellect are not in matter, they must be outside it.

Intellect- -One must be outside of such "order".

Intellect does not originate in soul, nor soul in body nor body in matter, but these emanate out of (the) One, and, with increasing degree of removal, express less of the (light of) (the) One – are less beautiful.

However, Plato almost touched on:
"Effect- -value, through, and indeed as, tension of relationship 'of forces', indefinite- -dynamic and inferentially multifaceted", **but** the step to a beautiful system was yet too great.

In his *Theaetetus* he considers that since 6 is greater than 4 and smaller than 12, 6 is both **great** and **small** and that since (low stature) Socrates is taller than a youth but one day will be shorter, he is both **tall** and **short**.

So Classical Philosophy expressed an incoherent dualism of Mother Nature (Matter) and Father Supernatural, and academic philosophers tweaked it, without satisfaction, apart from generated livelihood, power and prestige, for 2,400 years.

And when E-PS emerged; when they had something to endorse …

All the while technology developed and today, 2020, 25 years after E-PS emerged (25.12.1995), **primal intellect informed brain** is the operating software of (Western) Theists and Atheists alike.

In 2020 Primal Intellect Software wields Atom Bomb Brawn and various other means of world destruction.

Opportunity to upgrade the world from primal intellect informed formulation of the nature of things may not endure.

Cue: Most people require trendy cues for higher intellect to exert.

Effectuationism - Philosophy System (E-PS)

First Principle- -Premise: 'Perception'- -Perception.

(This has (of course) connotations of superposition wave function collapse, with which I am now more familiar: superposition indefinite- -dynamic state may potentially become- -collapse to more stable- -enduring form- -perception- -concept, albeit still indefinite- -dynamic).

The expressions 'Perception' and Perception may be substituted by Awareness or Being or Value or Energy or Matter or Effect or Tension, or Form, etc., as one pleases.

Perception- -Awareness, albeit elementary, inheres in- -as tension of indefinite- -dynamic sub-atomic 'forces'- -energy- -matter and potentially develops.

The single parenthesis 'Perception' develops into Perception, through **sufficient extent of recurrence** of tension of interaction- -relationship of 'forces'.

It is through 'somewhat recurrence' of tension of indefinite- -dynamic 'forces' that somewhat stable awareness- -concept emergence happens - tension of 'forces' never precisely recurs; indefinite- -dynamic tension of 'forces'.

That is, the single parenthesis Perception ('Perception') (or 'Being' or 'Matter' or whatever) denotes perception-

-form of tension of 'forces' that emerges but does not recur sufficiently to have continuous form- -perception- -concept, albeit indefinite- -dynamic.

However, with sufficient recurrence of option of form- -crystallisation- -collapse somewhat stabilised Perception- -Concept- -Form- -Energy- -Matter emerges, somewhat durably, and potentially endures and develops.

Perception- -Being- -Awareness- -Value- -Form- -Matter- -... through, and indeed as, tension of relationship of 'forces', indefinite- -dynamic and multifaceted.

Emphasis: **Universe, expressing Indefinite- -dynamic tension of relationship of 'forces', multifaceted; not categorical forms, except through primal intellect organisms facet.**

Second Principle:

Perception or Effect or Matter or Value, through, and indeed as, tension of relationship of 'forces', indefinite- -dynamic and inferentially multifaceted.

Emphasising: "Effect, through, and indeed as, tension of relationship of 'forces', indefinite- -dynamic and inferentially multifaceted".
("Effect": verb, non-referring).

Clearly, (the) emerging form am not the classical subject and object form (Nature), but somewhat first person, indefinite- - dynamic tension of 'forces', inferentially multifaceted and rather more holistic.

However, **for simplicity** in expressing this system I develop just one rather than a multiplicity of facets - of 'forces' expressing - albeit inferentially multifaceted.

As such effecting form am not in relationship with any other, even first person tense seems less appropriate than tense-less, albeit inferring other facets- -forms.

This system will not feature a mind-body distinction - the duality of Mother Nature and, shall we say, "Father Supernatural" - nor consequent incoherent causation and integration problems.

Further Principles:

Through, indeed as, indefinite- -dynamic tension of relationship of 'forces' somewhat recurring, perception- -concept- -energy- -matter- -form emerges, albeit initially indefinite superposition quantum 'forces'.

Some facets of the tensions remain more entangled; remain- -retain more perception- -tension- -concept; retain- -remain more indefinite- -dynamic - I- -Other.

They are en-route to biochemical organism rather than to less animate form.

Facets evolving to biological organisms change from expressing as indefinite- -dynamic I- -Other tension to feature sense of discrete I and Other in space and time.

Potentially, evolution would eventually produce high intellect faculty which would facilitate completion of the circle from I- -Other to I and Other and to I- -Other again, the latter, (in the West) through emergence of E-PS.

Emphasis: The circle, thereby, would have developed from quantum dynamics-like superposition of 'forces' to more formed- -collapsed perception- -concept- -form- -matter - to atomic and macro world state expressing more as definite, discrete, unchanging, categorical (**without condition**) phenomena - and then closing ('completing the circle') with high intellect inference formulating 'forces' and expressing the nature of things as: "Effect, through, and indeed as, tension of 'forces', indefinite- -dynamic and inferentially multifaceted.

A macro-world analogy of emergence and evolution:

Take the initial non-form (chaos) of strangers- -'forces' assembled for a disco dance. As the disco develops, formless 'forces' may gradually effect a group or groups; formless 'forces' **somewhat recur** and emerge- -form.

In effect, from non-form tensions, forms- -entities emerge- -effect, **though still indefinite- -dynamic.**

Such emerging indefinite- -dynamic forms would feature fluctuating tensions as to their centre of intensity.

Such indefinite forms featuring fluctuating tensions of centre of intensity would likely express tension as to the degree of flux of boundary of their respective form and forms – group or groups.

Any such developing indefinite- -dynamic form would be in on-going indefinite- -dynamic tension with other such 'forces' or developing forms, each with its somewhat unique tensions of relationships and evolving.

Demarcation~Interaction (D~I) nature of 'Nature' may express, in some instances, greater fluctuating indefinite- -dynamic tension than others.

Perhaps they would have potential for greater development and longer term survival but greater immediate risk of decline.

Perhaps more demarcated 'forces'- -matter, with more conservation of form and energy, would have less potential for development and vitality and less animation in their development.

In any case, through somewhat recurrence, various fluctuating forms- -perceptions- -concepts develop - some less animate and others more dynamic and complex.

The latter would feature more consciousness of development of themselves and their environment.

Biochemical organisms potentially emerge and develop.

Organisms emerging would initially be rather reflexive.

Reflex: Through indefinite- -dynamic 'forces' somewhat recurring **and developing**, coherent organisms effect.

Through tension with other 'forces', rather simple yes or no type reflexes express. Senses emerge.

An organism with a variety of senses gradually comes to feature inter-relation of the effecting reflexes- -identifications. A more advanced, complex organism emerges- -effects.

Central nervous system: A central nervous system, whereby various reflexes- -perceptions come into tension with each other at what become centres of integration, emerges. A plurality of such centres could generate centre of centres. In any case, centre emerges, albeit indefinite- -dynamic.

I or Ego: Perhaps thereby, **primal organisms** feature sense of I or Ego, as a somewhat stabile core, integrating primal sense data, albeit indefinite- -dynamic.

Primal Intellect: With further development, quite stabile nerves or senses evolve and, when acted upon, the sense- -intellect of quite definite and discrete- -categorical differences of forms in space and time emerges.

Sense of definite, stabile, categorical **"I" and "Other"** supersedes indefinite- -dynamic **I- -Other**.

Pressure increases for more and more data and therein for more and better (primal) nerves or senses, to fare better in a world of tension.

Memory: An interactive – central - nervous system would generate exponential increase of data, which would be somewhat recurring, and a faculty for memory potentially would emerge- -form and develop.

Relativity or rudimentary inference: Some relativity or rudimentary inference emerges, for example, that some food is very nourishing, but obtaining it involves much danger and exertion.

These three stages - reflexive, categorical and relative - seem to be apparent even in the modern human: in the baby, the child and the adolescent, respectively.

Cross-individual referral to third parties: Simple organisms propagate their kind. Such organisms would be interacting with each other, and referring each other- perhaps close family relatives - to what feature as definite, rather constant phenomena, which would include each other.

Language: To refer each other to third parties, for example a tree or a rock or a family member, they would be able to jointly observe such a third party, and to express to each other, to some extent, their respective concept 'of it'.

While 'it' would be a somewhat different concept for each, if any expressed their concept by a gesture or (vocal) sound and if the others tried to copy this expression then the first would have been impacted by their copied expression and, in turn, could acknowledge or confirm the expression by repeating it to them.

Thereby, they would develop the means by which to refer each other to 'third parties' - as distinct from identify with each other about stuff.

The capacity for more and better communication of concepts with each other would facilitate emergence of even greater quantity and complexity of (social) data.

Through somewhat recurring interaction, perhaps featuring more elaborate vocalisation or writing, sensitisation to the connotations of individual-particular concepts increases.

Constraints to (inter)action: 'Forces' in inter-relationship act or impact, to a degree, an account or connotations of themselves and the parties evolve in the process.

However, they are somewhat constrained because, e.g. of the suitability- -sensitivity of form of the second party to the action, concept or system being expressed.

'Forces' can also be constrained in (inter)acting through disruption by competing (inter)active forces, conflicts of interests, etc.

For example, the environment was probably more favourable to a new philosophy system twenty five years ago; there was much less electronic noise, the world was much calmer and there was much more interest in Philosophy; people had a sense of the software between their ears. Now focus is on that at their fingertips.

Multifaceted effects: The impact by a subject phenomenon upon that with which it is impacting, an object phenomenon, which, inferentially, in its own right is a subject phenomenon impacting with an object phenomenon, resolves.

This resolution is the consequently evolved subject phenomenon, or a facet of the subject phenomenon, in both parties. In effect, both would have evolved. They would perhaps infer that the interaction would have been a different event for each party. Low level inference gradually develops.

So, we do not identify with each other about stuff!

Low Intellect- -Inference: Through data accumulated through primal senses and memory, an organism **anticipates** probable resolutions of different impactions- -interactions and takes, e.g., evasive or remedial action, such as taking an indirect route to its nest or moving it to a new location, respectively, if suspecting danger.

Higher intellect- -inference: Inferentially developing more complex inter-related concepts.

High Intellect- -Inference: Awareness effecting of complex inter-related concepts, such as cultural 'knowledge', not fitting together very well and consequently pausing for data to accumulate anew in multiple inter-tensions and eventually resolving as new premises, concepts and system, perhaps as E-PS, and then coming into tension with the cultural system and, likewise, that tension resolving, with the cultural system (I and Other) becoming apparent as a system and perhaps being transcended (to I- -Other, again).

High intellect- -inference emergence: If not culturally proscribed from an early age, or perhaps constrained such as by pressure for rather exclusive exercise of primal intellect, higher intellect- -inference potentially emerges and develops and potentially would high-inferentially feature value as relational rather than categorical or relative – "Effect, through, and indeed as, tension of relationship of 'forces', indefinite- -dynamic and inferentially multifaceted".

Sense of I- -Other emerges again, completing a circle – perhaps something of a return to Mother Nature after long alienation- -incoherence.

Fate becomes high-inferential; high-inference features amongst 'forces' determining effectuation.

Higher and High Inference faring well: Trial and error inferential inter-relation of 'forces'- -data into different forms- -tensions potentially becomes culturally popular.

This has potential to boost dynamism in the sciences and life generally.

However, it would also have potential for unravelling of concepts- -value- -form to non-form – **D~I**.

Transcendence: Effectuation of value as relational and multifaceted, of oneself- -value- -form as indefinite- -dynamic I- -Other, superseding primal sense- -intellect of oneself as independent phenomenon, discrete, static, in space and time, expressing categorical I and categorical Other, and 'the Universe' as third party in space and time.

Potential for altruism: Through an elementary sense of I- -Other an animal altruistically attempts to protect its young or perhaps even others.

Similarly altruistically, Socrates preferred to sacrifice his biochemical form, through drinking hemlock, rather than renounce, and perhaps have lost to posterity, his intellectual pondering, often encapsulated as "I know nothing [categorically]" - which survived.

'Re-featuring': Data re-featuring from memory, rather than being an effect of non-memory featuring 'forces', would be a 'force' in a somewhat new set of non-memory 'forces', and would change in that tension of 'forces' before being memorised (again) in somewhat changed form, unless- -until faculty for inference features and perhaps contributes to preservation- -restoration of the opening form.

How re-featuring data fares in tension with fresh data probably depends on the level of the re-featuring data and that (fresh) with which it was coming into tension.

Re-featuring higher data might not fare well in tension with fresh (non-memory) sensory data of the moment.

However, it might fare better if the fresh data was higher intellect data.

For high intellect data, such as E-PS type data, to fare well in tension with re-featuring primal intellect data presumably would require that the recipient would be disposed to developing sensitivity to higher level data.

Summarising Inter-system tension: Classical Philosophy, through "poverty of [ ] ignorance", theorised incoherent, definite, static, discrete form, and that we universally identify with each other about such stuff but it was unable to integrate it with indefinite- -dynamic nature.

Through it we effect as aliens on Earth and largely at war with our **inherent** Mother Nature.

Classical categoricalist programming probably impedes high intellect- -inference emergence.

Perhaps one should not be surprised that through categoricalism there was little high intellect progress while brawn advanced amazingly.

Ethics: The individual as an individual in tension with the individual as a member of a community.

In the case of a society: the society as a society in tension with the society as a society amongst societies.

Democracy: A democratic political system should perhaps largely define as peaceful, consensual, egalitarian government of the people, by the people, for the people.

Presumably, the people would attempt to accommodate each other in their indefinite- -dynamic choices for their individual lives.

Democratically choosing people to, for example, direct the economy and national and inter-national affairs, albeit that the elected would in turn choose between different schools of thought on these issues, seems to be a rather risky system, involving the competence of the electorate and of the schools of thought and how the elected acquit themselves.

However, it seems preferable to alternative options; it is easier for citizens, upon changing their mind, to remove democratically elected politicians - if they are democrats.

Also the electorate knows that they chose the directors in the first instance and that those elected are probably an expression of the probably varying calibre of electorates; that the buck stops with them.

Presumably unsatisfactory choices would stir voters to smarten-up as voters faster than autocratic directors would self-improve or resign.

Democracy thereby seems more tolerant of indefinite- -dynamic value and of trial and error investigation and thereby is a better environment for development.

The price of liberty is eternal vigilance: Like all 'forces', liberty emerges through varying 'forces', including vigilance. This requires higher intellect exertion.

Justice: If we do not share a common world but instead are different facets of different tensions of 'forces' and if society's laws give rise to different dilemmas for each of us in our interrelation with those laws, then how is justice to be defined?

Well, we each know society's laws in advance of acting and in democracies we have a role in determining them - so they are factors in our determination- -acting.

If such determination brings one before the courts, one could advise the court of the forces at play for its consideration in determining a ruling.

Other Species: Like us they are conscious, self-aware and autonomy desiring. Perhaps we could at least become higher inferential enough to recognise it. Indeed perhaps they are higher inferential organisms.

Tension- -Consciousness: Somewhat recurring or familiar tension- -perception- -consciousness would not be as intense as would tension which is more novel; as tension of relationship of 'forces' resolves, tension- -perception- -consciousness declines.

Emotion: Organisms probably get used to a certain rate, or degree, of change as normal, above this as (high) emotion, and below it as boredom.

"Free v Determined": Value, through, and indeed as, tension of indefinite- -dynamic 'forces'.

As such, at any given moment of resolution, **one am expression of featuring multifaceted indefinite- -dynamic 'forces'**; not first party observer nor third party object.

One has some awareness of various facets in tension, albeit one am unable to anticipate entanglement- -development beyond a few 'steps'.

The incoherent, undefined notion of automatic decision making, inherent in Classical Philosophy does not, of course, feature in E-PS.

Fate- -Effectuation: Through development of higher and high inference, one becomes a more complex factor to evolving Mother Nature, making Mother Nature more evolved- -advanced henceforth.

A faculty for high inference emerging as a factor- - 'force', at both individual and universal levels, may be a great effectuation of fate.

High intellect- -inference expressing can be a determining factor in fate henceforth, making fate henceforth more high intellect- -inference effectuating.

Perhaps this under-estimates awareness- -entanglement at Quantum Dynamics level.

A Classical issue: Why is there something rather than nothing? Again, categoricals – such as "something" and "nothing" - do not arise through or feature in E-PS. E-PS expresses: effect, through … 'forces'.

Happiness: The belief that one is making progress, or contemplation of progress made, towards one's objectives.

Evolved form- -value- -effect- -I: Having conceptualised this new formulation of the nature of things, it would come into tension with one's prior featuring formulation- -system.

The tension would resolve - one thriving and the other declining.

Of course, given many readers conceptualizing E-PS, there

would be a multiplicity of facets - of the nature of things - in tension with E-PS, generating a multiplicity of effecting conceptualizations, which then come into tension with their respective prior systems, generating a multiplicity of tensions and resolutions.

Indefinite- -dynamic multifaceted nature would remain so.

However, potentially forces in tension would be less categorical and higher inferential.

Presumably evolved form would be more democracy, diversity and nature friendly, perhaps something of a return to multifaceted entanglement.

Buddhism may have connotations in common with E-PS and perhaps also Voltaire in the Candide: "Throb thine with Nature's throbbing breast, and all is clear from east to west".

Note: For simplicity in developing E-PS, I featured just one facet, rather than a multiplicity of facets evolving differently - of facets of 'forces' expressing - albeit form **inferentially** multi-faceted, and so one facet implicitly connotes perhaps all facets.

Effectuationism Grid System (EGS)

EGS is E-PS informed.

It is a (rudimentary) alternative positioning system to Albert Einstein's "On the Electrodynamics of Moving Bodies" – The Theory of Special Relativity.

The Effectuationism Grid System (EGS) is basically a Cartesian co-ordinate system with a standard event speed (SES), such as rotation (on its axis) of the Earth in relation to the Sun and expressed as 1440 Minutes or a Caesium-133 atomic clock which uses the transition frequency between two energy states of the atom.

A rocket or satellite can develop an x,y,z grid.
Let's call it Frame-rocket (F-r), necessarily of co-ordinates x0, y0, z 0 (0, 0, 0).

Provide it with sensors- -eyes.

Arrange that a body, such as Earth, has co-ordinates in the F-r grid. F-r can be in geo-static or moving relationship to the body - Earth.

With the provided sensors, let F-r arrange that a distinctive feature on Earth recurs at regular intervals. F-r can arrange to map the movement of that distinctive feature in its grid.

If the feature is moving, to map its path F-r would arrange to have 'eyes' or rockets at some remove from itself, forming loops around Earth, their co-ordinates known and updated as necessary, facilitated by triangulation.

Arranging such a system, F-r would require relationship with ground beacons (or two other rockets), whereby they can 'see' each other and thereby the three axes of F-r can be stable (non-rotating on their intersecting axes), to generate rather familiar world effect and can establish one as the x-axis and the other as y-axis.

Elaborating: A frame, even if only a point or a rocket, in relationship with a body, such as Earth, can choose to have its, let's say, "positive z-axis" from itself to and through the body and its negative z-axis going from itself in the opposite radial direction. It can have two further axes, x and y, at right angles to each other and to z, with all three intersecting at (0, 0, 0).

Having established x, y and z axes, the Frame rocket (F-r) can arrange that the distinctive feature on Earth is someplace in its positive z-axis, at value 0 on its y–axis and rotating in its x-axis.

As it moves out of view of F-r it moves into view of other rockets which have given and updated positions in the grid. Its circular movement in the grid can be mapped.

For example, let it commence as x_0, y_0 and z_1 (0, 0, 1). (It is directly in front of F-r's intersecting axes, but out a bit). The y value is constant, but the feature moves in the x-axis, let's say, rotating from West to East; from -x to +x, much as per the Sun. Simultaneous to its movement into +x co-ordinates it moves increasingly into +z co-ordinates, then progressing to its maximum in +x while still increasing in +z and on to x0 and to maximum in +z, then on to maximum in -x as it decreases to its medium in +z, and then on to x0 and z1 again.

Let R-b be at F-r co-ordinate (-3, 0, 1), seeing Earth - perhaps another belt of it, if the system is geo-centric - as out perhaps 0.9 in its z axis (-3, 0, 0.9). Effectively this feature would be in F-r co-ordinate (-3, 0, 1.9).

The position or trajectory and velocity of various other 'eyes'- -rockets and loops of rockets can be monitored in the grid.

F-r, using light pulses, its clock (SES) can synchronise with clocks on any rockets it can directly 'see'. These clocks can synchronise with clocks they can 'see', thereby establishing how far one is from another and any rate of movement.

Any synchronization of clocks simply involves bringing secondary clocks into agreement - sync - with F-r's clock, based on the round trip (each way) light signals - effectively synchronization of measurements of light speed between clocks.

F-r can synchronise its clock with that of Rocket-b (R-b) by having R-b clock accord with F-r's measurement of the **round trip** speed of a light signal from F-r to R-b when it (R-b) measures its pulses to F-r and back.

This requires that if R-b has any speed- -velocity in relation to F-r it will be stable or stably changing.

F-r's clock can then, directly or indirectly and by the same light-over-distance-means, synchronise with yet another R clock, such as R-c's, which it can see, and which in turn can see R-b. Indeed, R-b and R-c can verify that they are in sync, by light signals to and from each other.

All clocks in the system can synchronise.

They would also monitor that they remain in sync and indeed syncronised with the Standard Event Speed (SES).

An event in relationship **with the clock** of any rocket, say R-d, would effect as the When or Minute of the (1440) SES cycle and, if it is a travelling event, its speed is d/u - avoiding the t-word.

As the position of all rockets is monitored, if the position and rate of velocity of a rocket, such as R-d is changing slightly in the grid, it and all other rockets know its position.

Such possibly changing velocity of R-d has no bearing on the speed its clock (u) calculates for an event travelling in the grid, as it is the clock (SES or a mechanical proxy for it) **inertial in the clock shell** (in the rocket shell) **that is the frame for how long, units (u) of SES, the event takes – the travelling of a distance.**

If transmitting this information to another rocket, allowance for the distance and rate of travel of the information could be made.

Whether a clock in a different gravitation field to the main system of rockets would be sufficiently inure in its inertial shell to be unaffected by the novel gravity, I leave open.

Whether this also applies as regards to novel velocity, I leave open.

An accelerating rocket, necessarily in the grid, perhaps remote from the main system: its trajectory and velocity would be known throughout the system, as necessary – and so its information would be understandable.

Such a rocket observing an event in its zone, would easily observe its trajectory and velocity – given that it knows its own.

Summary:

E-PS features only one frame in its grid system, so no frame hopping.

Classical Time is substituted by SES.

Space is substituted _not_ by "the grid" nor even by "a grid" but by "Frame", which implies (a) grid.

Concluding with extracts from and comments on Albert Einstein's "**On the Electrodynamics of Moving Bodies**":
"It may appear that all difficulties connected with the definition of time can be removed when in place of time, we substitute the position of the little hand of my watch. Such a definition is in fact sufficient, when it is required to define time exclusively for the place at which the clock is stationed. But the definition is not sufficient when it is required to connect by time events taking place at different stations, — or what amounts to the same thing,— to estimate by means of time (zeitlich werten) the occurrence of events, which take place at stations distant from the clock."

Re "Such a definition is in fact sufficient, when it is required to define time exclusively for the place at which the clock is stationed. **But the definition is** not sufficient when it is required to connect by time **events taking place at different stations, ...**":

E-PS- -EGS: A clock is an indicator of **units (u)**, such as minutes, of some standard (SES), such as spin on its axis of Earth in relation to the Sun.

Synchronised clocks signifying ticks of units (u) of some standard event speed **are the frame for when – "connect by time"** - **events happen.**

Velocity of the clock, its mechanisms inertial in its clock shell, is irrelevant, except for any contraction of matter effects.

Speed of an event is d/u.

29.May.1919 Sun Eclipse and Hyades Light...

I. Newton:"...even though they are defined differently, gravitational mass [F = G*m1*m2/r^2] and inertial mass [F = ma] always seem to be equal".

Force (F) of G: gravitation m1m2: kg.kg, inverse square law of distance r^2, e.g. if distance trebles, F declines by 9, if it quadruples, F declines by 16.

For the 29.May.1919 Eclipse, Newtonian scholars predicted a certain amount of curvature of light from Hyades passing near the Sun. Albert Einstein, in The Theory of General Relativity, predicted twice as much, and became famous when the observations better accorded with his absurd modelling.

To produce a system, albeit after many years of torment endured, that prevails in tension with the competition, it must feature more rigorous data or more rigorous concepts.

Equations F = G*m1*m2/r^2 and F = ma preceded A.E. by two hundred years.

Newton's concepts- -formulas may have prompted A.E. to include an inertial (i) value of m2 (i of light prior to interaction with the Sun) - albeit the way (w) of (i) was not towards dead center of the Sun, so say: **0.9p** (9/10p).

So, including i of m2 into **Newtonian formula**:
F = G*m1*(m2+(wi))/r^2 .

A.E. imagined himself riding alongside a star-light-beam.

I suspect it occurred to him that the photon stream entered with velocity the Sun's significant attraction field- -force.

Newtonian scholars probably never calculated for it.

Einstein probably did, using his S.R. premises and concepts of light, empty space, time dilation and non-instantaneous gravity. He would then have had equations complimenting his SR.

If he used S.R. concepts, the revolutionary, absurd modelling and his presentation of it may have been genuine – he may have been too exhausted to realise it could be modelled in I.N. concepts - in which case the acclaim he received may have been deserved - or it was a strategy to cohere with and protect S.R.

If he had used I.N. modelling, his contribution to science might have been acknowledged (though I would not count on it, given my own experiences) but it would have conflicted with his SR concepts; concepts of S.R. and I. N. systems would not cohere.

Shock at the radical system, 'inference' of a Maxwell basis, claim of the system preceding the data and of seven years of torment might have dissuaded people from applying I.N. concepts.

(The value of the precession of the perihelion of Mercury was established by S. Newcomb in 1895 and I suspect could have been relativistically modelled by A.E. to show that value).

Arthur Eddington parody of The Rubaiyat of Omar Khayyam about his famed 1919 expedition:
Oh leave the Wise our measures to collate
One thing at least is certain, LIGHT has WEIGHT,
One thing is certain, and the rest debate –
Light-rays, when near the Sun, DO NOT GO STRAIGHT.
A.E.: "One thing I have learned in a long life: that all our science, measured against reality, is primitive and childlike – and yet it is the most precious thing we have."

Emergence- -Electro-magnetism- -Gravity

... and then, (under pressure - greater entanglement) in the first seconds of Big Bang through photons- -vibrations- -spins of electro-magnetism colliding, protons, neutrons and electrons emerged. In the following seconds, of the first perhaps three minutes, protons collided and formed ions of Hydrogen and Helium and some Lithium. After cooling for 380,000 years electrons were captured- -bound and atoms emerged; Universe of Hydrogen (H) (75%) and Helium (He) (25) (and trace amount of Lithium (Li)) emerged through - inferring from current theories of these atoms – electro-magnetism forces such as photon energy units- -quanta – which under their own pressure big-banged, generating sufficient heat for perhaps three minutes to generate a universe of H and He ions and, with 380,000 years of cooling, H, He and Li atoms.

These elements express- -feature dualities - the duality of electro-magnetism and the duality of photon wave-particle.

Atoms consist of a nucleus and one or more electrons.

These features of an atom are in tension with each other and rather stable at a certain remove- -pressure.

Electron(s) vibrate- -spin at some remove- -pressure from its/their atomic nucleus, in a world of such atoms- -elements.

So an atom is a dynamic phenomenon and probably featuring inherent dualisms – inter-dependent tensions of forces.

Universe would be a world of such inter-dependent tensions of vibrating- -spinning forces, featuring what we call Gravity.

Subsequent clustering- -vibrating- -pressuring of such atoms bang as Suns …, fusing them and generating further atoms up to the level of Iron (Fe) during the life of such Suns and in the last two seconds of their lives as the pressure at core builds until it pressures, collapses and explodes- -bangs the remaining atoms of the periodic table are formed and scattered … perhaps to …

Perhaps the Big Bang expansion of the Universe and its subsequent development may cause sufficient weakening of tension- -entanglement between some bodies – perhaps galaxies - that they drift and perhaps the drift accelerates …

Note: I recommend that in modelling of Quantum Dynamics one should abandon the concepts: observer and space and time. Instead inform modelling with E-PS, such as the principle: Effect, through, and indeed as, tension of relationship of 'forces', indefinite- -dynamic and inferentially multi-faceted.

Mathematics

I find that Mathematics is an extension of language; a way to express great detail efficiently- -economically. For example, to express the quantity 100, one could say 1 + 1 +1 + 1 ... (or i,i,i,i, ... as the Romans did) whereas modern math (language) can simply do so with 100.

Language and gestures express or refer concepts.

Concepts are system particular. For example, elephants holding up the world in Flat Earth Cosmology, none in Helio-centric Cosmology, rather momentum and gravity.

So, if one is expressing a new system one is expressing new concepts – particular to that new system.

Therefore the math of another system – math which expresses concepts particular to a different system – have ZERO role in expression of the new system.

However, the terminology and symbols and gestures may be employed, but for entirely new referrals.

For example, my formula for speed: $s = d/u$.

ECCE

Advances in modelling sub-atomic indefinite- -dynamic tensions of 'forces', together with micro-technology innovation which facilitates their manipulation- -engineering, promises a yield of economic clean controllable energy (ECCE) (perhaps first in N-S).

Off topic 1 - "Beam me up, Scotty"

If we master super-position wave function collapse, we may soon-after master reversing it, effectively realizing the "Beam me up, Scotty" idea.

Off topic 2 – Fate

I was trying to recall, when writing to publish on a somewhat different subject (D,P,R) why I had **not** got back to Prof. B.E. O'Mahony, who had given a positive analysis 14.07.1993 (Scan 1). I **in**correctly speculated a reason. I had found around year 2,005 that E-PS needed a specialist platform; that most people require trendy cues for higher intellect to exert.

I now recall the reason: I had placed his reply to me and the envelope in which it arrived within a reply envelope from Prof. D.M., in which for some years there had been a second reply letter from D.M. and which at some stage I removed, and when looking for it - O'M's - I overlooked it as mail from O'M.
Years later I found it but Prof. O'M was then deceased. Fate!

Effectuationism - Philosophy-Physics
(E P-P) (Oct 2020)

E-PS substituted for Classical Philosophy

EGS substituted for Special Relativity

$F = G\, m_1\, (m_2+(wi))/r^2$ equation- -idea substituted for GR

E-PS coheres with Quantum Dynamics - may inform modelling

Gravity: Entangled universe of inter-dependent tensions of forces.

Grand Cohering Theories

Monetary and Trade Theory

A currency first of all **represents** the tradable wealth of the society using it - Y units currency : X wealth - and is a medium of inter-change - of wealth.

Given stability of Y:X, it also is a store of wealth- -value.

A society should be very vigilant about the extent to which unit-money-value is manipulated, e.g., as a means of controlling how wealth behaves; the extent to which it rests, or is risked, and the form in which it is invested- -risked and of its redistribution- -transfer.

These factors are determinants of how tradeable wealth of a society, as distinct from units of money, grows long term.

They would also seem to be determinants of the freedom and creativity of the individual in society and of the society generally and consequently of its development.

Trade: Trade is, for example, when one party has an extra horse and the second party an extra cow and the first wants a cow and the second a horse or one party has one form of wealth for sale and another party has another e.g. labour and so they each sell- -trade.

Thereby a society's economy develops and the wealth remains in the community of participants. Also societies trade with each other.

It would seem that the different parties should subscribe to the same model- -system of how trade and currency operates – coherence.

If they have different systems, there is predisposition to incoherence.

In the mid-1990s I was aware of theories (presented at conference) that much of the developed world economy should be migrated--transferred to the impoverished world which would do the manufacturing and sell the products to the developed world and the latter would innovate and sell new advanced products to the former. These "Globalization" ideas seemed badly thought out, other than if intended as assistance as distinct from the traditional idea of trade, or were designed for individual national or corporate self-interest.

Such economic policies would be a dramatic shift from gradual inter-society organic building of economies and inter-national trade.

There was no awareness expressed about the **rate of transition** nor whether the transfer of manufacturing would happen faster than innovation nor of how a society would innovate if its factories were closed down and it was not tinkering with technology, nor, even if it did innovate, how quickly the generated production opportunities would move to the former nor about impact on the current system.

Chances seemed slim of competition keeping trade in balance and the developed world solvent and its population in jobs if the wealth and know-how was **rapidly** transferred to a much larger and, due to recent social experiment, much, much poorer society, with very different human rights standards and much more centrally directed, facilitating stealthy State advantages to sectors of its choosing - different **system**.

The developed world would soon become exhausted. The recipient economy would need to quickly become self-reliant or it would follow the other into crisis. Relations would be stressed and difficult to resolve. **There is also the issue of a free system strengthening non-free.**

These theories were operated with little general public engagement.

Likewise **the developed world also seems in crisis due to** not having transcended old and new - Theistic & Atheistic - intellect of the primal senses informed ideologies, **specialists apparently preferring to slink away on emergence of E-PS rather than openly address it.**

Scan 1: "... it is too long and complicated for any detailed analysis. Even a cursory glance would indicate that it would take years to unravel the major philosophical issues you raise and to assess the weight and originality of the arguments presented. I would not know where to start; and ... I don't know what advice to offer. ..."

Coláiste na hOllscoile Corcaigh, Éire
University College Cork, Ireland

ROINN NA FEALSÚNACHTA
Department of Philosophy

14 July 1993

Mr Peter Kinane,
Ballywalter,
Dundrum,
Co. Tipperary.

Dear Mr Kinane,

Thank you for your enquiry (referred to me by the Faculty Office).

Having read quickly through your work entitled *Perception*, I must reply that it is too long and complicated for any detailed analysis. Even a cursory glance would indicate that it would take years to unravel the major philosophical issues you raise and to assess the weight and originality of the arguments presented. I would not know where to start; and I doubt if anything I could say would simply improve the MS.

I don't know what advice to offer. I have consulted with another member of the Philosophy staff here at University College, Cork (Professor D. Clarke) and he is equally at a loss as to what he could do.

With regrets for being of no help to you,

I remain,

Yours sincerely,

B.E.O'Mahony

Brendan E. O'Mahony
Professor of Philosophy & Head of Department

Scan 2: "This Paper was not available ...": I suspect that upon my publishing and making available to conference organizers my new system in Jan. 1996 there was a late switch to safety and irrelevance from Putnam ("Realism") to Wittgenstein to avoid embarrassment, not leaving time for a reply paper before pre-publishing of July 1996 papers. At the conference **the hosts, and all in-the-know**, proceeded to discuss my work, uncredited, e.g., "What does it say about the great minds over the centuries?".

ON WITTGENSTEIN'S PHILOSOPHY OF MATHEMATICS

Hilary Putnam and James Conant

II—*James Conant*

This paper was not available at the time of going to press. It will be published in a future volume of the Proceedings of The Aristotelian Society.

B-H Evening Scene

View

E P-P

E-PS: Higher intellect premises supersede intellect of the primal senses premises informing a new Philosophy-Physics.

Second Principle: Effect, through, and indeed as, tension of relationship of 'forces', indefinite- -dynamic and inferentially multi-faceted. ("Effect": verb, non-referring)

Ethics: The individual as an individual in tension with the individual as a member of a community.

E P-P: A profound Philosophy-Physics higher intellect read.

Quote from Voltaire Candide: "Throb thine with Nature's throbbing breast, and all is clear from east to west".

ISBN: 978-0-9954548-8-0

Most people require trendy cues for higher intellect to exert. ...

Made in the USA
Coppell, TX
12 August 2021